For my brother, who knows his way around a bad idea — RP

For Wes, a budding naturalist — KD

Paperback edition published by Tundra Books, 2023

TEXT COPYRIGHT © 2022 BY RACHEL POLIQUIN
ILLUSTRATIONS COPYRIGHT © 2022 BY KATHRYN DURST

Tundra Books, an imprint of Tundra Book Group, a division of Penguin Random House of Canada Limited

LIBRARY AND ARCHIVES CANADA CATALOGUING IN PUBLICATION

Title: How to high tea with a hyena (and not get eaten) / Rachel Poliquin ; illustrated by Kathryn Durst.
Names: Poliquin, Rachel, 1975- author. | Durst, Kathryn, illustrator.
Identifiers: Canadiana 20220172919 | ISBN 9781774881668 (softcover)
Subjects: LCSH: Hyenas—Juvenile literature.
Classification: LCC QL737.C24 P65 2023 | DDC j599.74/3—dc23

Published simultaneously in the United States of America by Tundra Books of Northern New York, an imprint of Tundra Book Group, a division of Penguin Random House of Canada Limited

LIBRARY OF CONGRESS CONTROL NUMBER: 2020951915

Edited by Elizabeth Kribs
Designed by John Martz

The artwork in this book was created using pencil crayons and finished digitally.
The text was set in set in typefaces based on hand lettering by Kathryn Durst.

PRINTED IN CHINA

www.penguinrandomhouse.ca

1   2   3   4   5   27   26   25   24   23

Penguin
Random House
tundra | TUNDRA BOOKS

How to High Tea with a Hyena

(And Not Get Eaten)

RACHEL POLIQUIN

ILLUSTRATED BY KATHRYN DURST

tundra

HELLO!

It's me, Celeste!
I'm a COCKROACH.

That means I'm a

SURVIVOR.

Me and my kind
have been around for
300 MILLION
YEARS!

But I'm not *just* a survivor.
I come from a long line of
CLASSY survivors.

DAPPER,
Dashing,
tasteful
& graceful.

That's me!

3

AND I CAN
TEACH YOU.

Not just how to outsmart an ordinary

ALLIGATOR or
BEADY-EYED BABOON
but how to SURVIVE the

POLITE PREDATORS

in your life, the sly ones

that invite you for

TEA ON THE
TERRACE or
POKER IN THE
PARLOR.

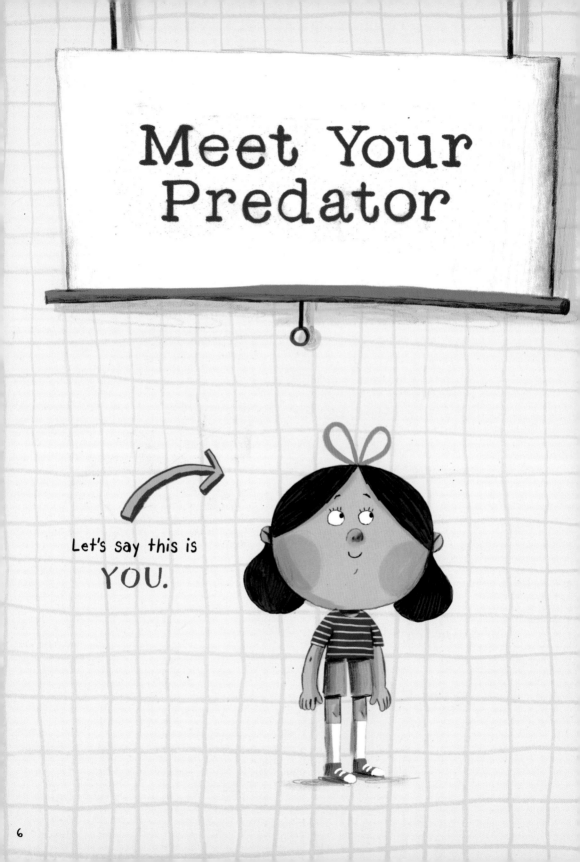

Meet Your
Predator

Let's say this is
YOU.

And let's say this is a
ONE-HUNDRED-SIXTY-POUND
hyena named RUBY.

And let's say one afternoon,
Ruby says to you,
"ABE (or **ABINA** or
WHATEVER your name is),

It's
4 O'CLOCK
and my tummy is
GRUMBLING.

Care to **JOIN ME** for **HIGH TEA?"**

Now, I know HIGH TEA is a dainty meal
with tiny sandwiches and pretty teacups.

And you know a HYENA
is a wild animal.

So I'm sure we both know high tea with
a hyena is probably a BAD IDEA.

But I like bad ideas, especially
VERY BAD IDEAS.

And right in the middle of this especially bad idea are two deliciously **TRICKY PROBLEMS.**

Tricky Problem #1: Ruby isn't dainty. She doesn't sip — she slobbers. She doesn't nibble — she gnaws. She has never used a napkin in her life.

Tricky Problem #2: Ruby is a ferocious hunter. She could gobble you up faster than this jam tart. And that's a problem. In fact, some might say it's **THE** problem.

I'm beginning to think
HIGH TEA WITH A HYENA
might be the **WORST** idea anyone has ever had.

I say, "**YES PLEASE!**"

So let's you and me get down to business and figure out how to have high tea with a hyena (and not get eaten).*

*Please **NEVER** try any of this at home, because this is all a very bad idea.

STEP ONE:
Pick Your
Hyena

There are four kinds of hyenas, and they all live in Africa. There are striped hyenas, spotted hyenas, brown hyenas and the aardwolf, which is more like an aardvark than a wolf or a hyena. It's smallish, skittery and eats only bugs.

Ruby is a SPOTTED HYENA,
and spotted hyenas are the biggest and fiercest of all.
As tall as Great Danes and built like bulldogs, spotted hyenas
can weigh as much as 32 CHIHUAHUAS.

YAP
YAP
YAP

(Just so you know, although hyenas look a bit like
dogs, they are definitely NOT dogs.
They are most closely related to
MONGOOSES,
which look a bit like
weasels but aren't.)

And Ruby isn't just ANY spotted hyena.
She is the queen and leader of her clan and the
BIGGEST, TOUGHEST hyena around.
Female hyenas are the bosses, and they mean business.

You might like to invite an aardwolf to tea instead.
But I think that's a TERRIBLE idea.
An aardwolf wouldn't like the
ham sandwiches or my famous
cream buns. Plus, I've heard
NASTY RUMORS that
aardwolves eat cockroaches
like popcorn. And popcorn
has no place at a
tea party.

I'm sure Ruby will make an EXCELLENT tea guest.

Spotted hyenas are ALWAYS hungry
and will eat almost ANYTHING.

Large feasts or dainty bites,
fresh or not-so-fresh,
as long as there is some meat on
or near or under the table,
RUBY IS READY TO DINE.

Besides, when planning a party,
it's always important to consider the
WORST-CASE SCENARIO.
And a hungry hyena named Ruby is about
AS BAD AS IT GETS.

KNOW YOUR HYENA:

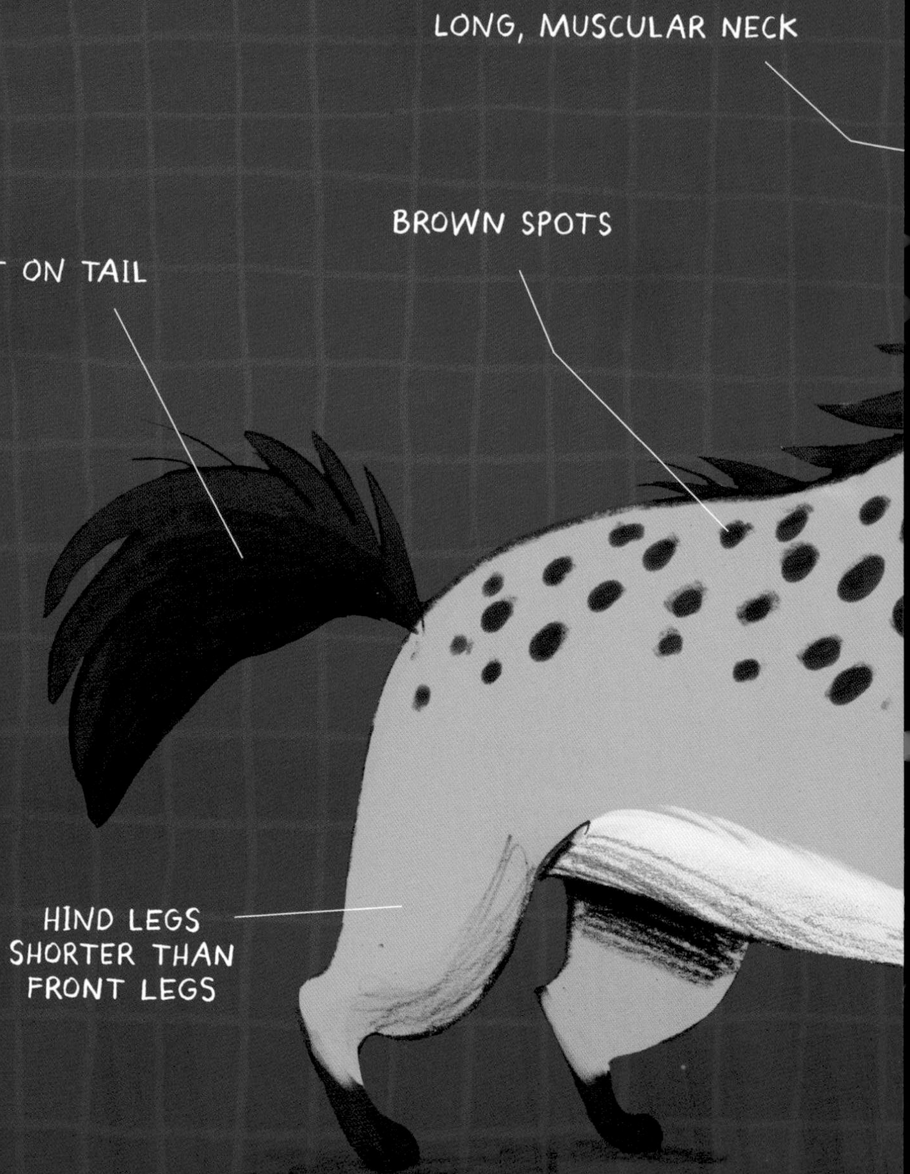

LONG, MUSCULAR NECK

BROWN SPOTS

TUFT ON TAIL

HIND LEGS
SHORTER THAN
FRONT LEGS

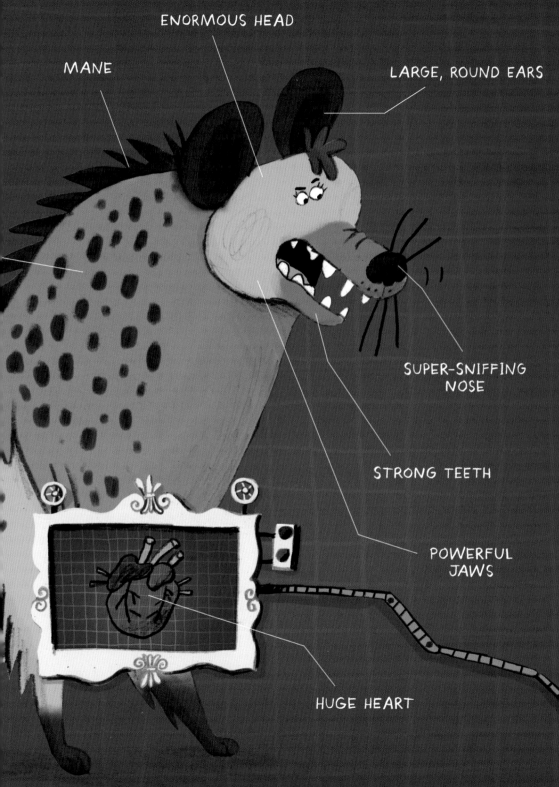

ENORMOUS HEAD

MANE

LARGE, ROUND EARS

SUPER-SNIFFING
NOSE

STRONG TEETH

POWERFUL
JAWS

HUGE HEART

STEP TWO:
Dress Nicely

High tea can be a feast, but it isn't REALLY a meal.
It's more of an afternoon date with close friends.
You nibble tiny cakes, sip milky tea and chitchat about
not-so-important things like whether skunks make good
pets, if fish have eyebrows and why donuts have holes.

Before we can do any of that, let's
find you something to wear.

Nothing too fancy or formal, but shorts are DEFINITELY NOT classy enough. You should look POLITE and PROPER. I'm thinking a tea dress with a bit of lace, a few ruffles, maybe a ribbon at the waist.

This one with the high collar and long sleeves is perfect. It's probably wise to keep skin covered when eating with a hyena.

And how about a hat? You can never go wrong with a plume.

Don't you look DIVINE!

Ruby is quite dashing, just as she is.
Her golden fur and spots are
CHIC and STYLISH,
and that tufty tail
is downright
JAUNTY!

We'll meet her in the conservatory.

I set everything out earlier.
I made ham triangles, deviled eggs,
cucumber sandwiches, smoked salmon rolls,
my FAMOUS cream buns . . .

This is **DEFINITELY NOT** dainty!
Where is her napkin?
And did she eat
ALL the buns?

Ruby has broken
the two golden rules
of high tea.

Rule #1: Don't gobble up the
cakes before your guests arrive.
Only slightly less important is
Rule #2: Never, EVER
stand on the table.

We need to teach Ruby
some manners.

STEP THREE:
Take Dainty Bites

HUNGRY LION

HUNGRY LEOPARD

Here is our problem: hyenas are very, **VERY** fast eaters. They have good reason — they need to eat **AS MUCH AS POSSIBLE AS FAST AS THEY CAN** before a leopard or lion tries to steal their dinner.

A hyena can eat 30 pounds (13.5 kg) in 30 minutes and, apparently, an entire high tea in 5 minutes flat.

HIGH-SPEED GOBBLING

makes good sense in the wild, but it's a **DEFINITE NO-NO** in the tearoom.

First, a fast eater is a messy eater.
Just look at Ruby's face! Second, everyone knows
you should NEVER speak with your mouth full.

Why? Because GOBBLING
means no chitchat.

No jokes. No stories.
NO GOSSIP!

PSSSSTT...

And where's the fun in THAT?

Take it from me, nothing makes a
cucumber sandwich taste quite as delicious as
a little TITTLE-TATTLE on the side.

What we need is a
SPECIAL DELIVERY SYSTEM
to make sure Ruby eats only one cake at a time.

CHOO CHOO!

I have just the thing —
A TRAIN SET!
I have the one my
Uncle Billy rode every
day to work.

Here's what we need to do:

1. SET UP TRACKS.

Connect the tracks to go around the room.

2. ARRANGE TEA.

I'll put the tea on this trolley.

3. PLACE BUNS AND POUR TEA.

Your job is to place one bun on a train every time it circles around. And don't forget to refill Ruby's teacup.

WONDERFUL!

This is working better than expected.
You've both mastered the art of dainty eating.
Now let's practice the chitchat.

STEP FOUR:
Gossip

As the queen of her clan, Ruby always has a lot to say. In fact, spotted hyenas are some of the CHATTIEST animals around. Their clans can be very large — with over 100 HYENAS.

As you probably know, the larger the family, the more there is to discuss. Mealtime, playtime, bedtime, party-time, teatime . . . everything needs organizing.

Spotted hyenas GROWL GROAN WHOOP yip RUMBLE SNARL Squeal and squitter.

They WHOOP to bring the clan together from miles around.

They RUMBLE when danger is near.

HEE HEE HEE

They GROAN and SQUEAL when they meet each other.

They even have a nervous GIGGLE.

Spotted hyenas are sometimes called LAUGHING HYENAS because of that giggle, although they only giggle when anxious or overly excited.

HEH-HEH...

Ruby doesn't speak human. So you'll have to learn hyena. Just repeat EVERYTHING she says.

And remember: Ruby is queen of her clan — make sure you giggle nervously and eat less than her. That way she'll know you know SHE'S THE BOSS.

This is going
SPLENDIDLY!

I thought high tea
with a hyena would be
DANGEROUS.
But I'm having a
wonderful time!

Did you hear something?

I thought I heard a yip.

That was **DEFINITELY** a whoop!

HEEEE

HEEEE

HEEEEE...

Goodness me ... it's RUBY'S FAMILY!

They weren't invited! We don't
have enough seats for everyone.
Or enough sandwiches!

She really should have let us
know they were coming.

But we have a bigger problem —
hyenas don't just live together.
They HUNT together.

I'm beginning to think that Ruby isn't interested in
my cream buns and a little gossip. I think Ruby
and her clan may just be HUNGRY.

DON'T PANIC!

I'm not saying she **does** want to eat you.
But I'm not saying she **doesn't**.

Just put all the buns on that train and back away,
SLOWLY and CAREFULLY.

STEP FIVE:
Know the Attack

I have GOOD NEWS and BAD NEWS.

The good news is that most people think hyenas are scavengers, which means they only eat already-dead dinners they've stolen. That means you would be safe-ish.

The bad news is that most people are wrong. Spotted hyenas kill 90 percent of their meals. In fact, lions and leopards steal more dinners from hyenas than the other way around.

That means you are

DEFINITELY
NOT safe.

Hyenas eat everything: wildebeest, warthogs, foxes, zebras, porcupines, goats, gazelles . . . I could go on.

Menu
Zebra
Fox
Rabbit
Goat
Warthog

They hunt different meals in different ways.
Small dinners — like rabbits — are
usually hunted alone. Large dinners
— like zebras — are
family events.

You're bigger than a rabbit but smaller than a zebra,
so I'm not sure how Ruby would hunt you.

But since her clan is
here, let me describe
the HERD
HUNTING
TECHNIQUE.

I'll use this
PIÑATA
to explain. It's very
festive, don't you think?

1. THE LURK:

DINNER

PIÑATAS

Hyenas will lurk around the edge of a herd of dinner,
just **WATCHING** and **WAITING.**

Dinner knows the hyenas are there,
but they don't pay much attention.
There is always safety in numbers.

2. THE LOPE AND SCOPE:

One or two hyenas will slowly run through the herd, just to check out what's what. Maybe they're looking for small dinners or dinners with a limp.

SNIFF
SNIFF
SNIFF

It's sort of like you wandering up and down the aisle of a candy store, just to see what's for sale.

BOINK

3. THE BREAKAWAY:

A sudden breakaway happens.
Perhaps a hyena made the first move,
or maybe dinner got jumpy and
decided to run. Either way,

THE CHASE IS ON.

SUPER FAST

4. THE CHASE:

Often just one hyena will chase until dinner gets tired. Hyenas are fast and can run forever.

5. THE TEAR AND GOBBLE:

Everyone gets in on the action.
Hyenas have mouths full of pointy teeth, and they use
their powerful neck muscles to tear big chunks.

OH MY! Look at those candies fly!

Hyenas aren't tidy eaters. They don't swallow you whole like a python. (Between you and me, pythons are ESPECIALLY tricky and not to be trusted.)

But hyenas are tidy. They eat the ENTIRE dinner, and FAST. Before you've turned around twice, the biggest of dinners will be 100 percent gone, tassels and all.

Amazing, right? But awful, too.

CHOMP
CHOMP

Just
AWFUL
and
TERRIBLE,
especially if it
happened to you.

MUNCH
MUNCH
MUNCH

We need a plan.
And I've got a
GREAT IDEA.

STEP SIX:
Invite Slow Friends

Don't even think about trying to outrun Ruby.
Hyenas can run 30 miles (50 km) an hour, which is
faster than you can ride a bike.

Even if you could run that fast, hyenas are endurance
hunters. Their short hind legs and long necks give them a
SUPER energy-efficient lope, and their enormous
hearts give them ENDLESS stamina.

They could keep running long after dinner
is caught, if they needed to.

However, maybe you don't need to be fast to survive. My Aunty Minnie used to say,

"You don't need to outrun the bear. You just need to outrun **YOUR FRIEND.**"

It's a terrible saying — forget I said it. But Aunty Minnie makes a good point. If we surround you with lots of SLOW FRIENDS, Ruby might choose one of them instead. Remember, there is always SAFETY IN NUMBERS.

SO HERE IS MY PLAN:

1. Collect as many friends as you can find.

Make sure your friends are
smaller and cuter than you. Hyenas
don't often go for zebra stallions
— too DANGEROUS!

You'll look HUGE
and FIERCE
compared to this
PINK
UNICORN.

2. Hide in the middle of the herd.

Excellent! You are perfectly surrounded by
TASTY-LOOKING cuteness. But
we have a problem. High tea is supposed to be a
small gathering with a few close friends — not a
HUGE PARTY!

WORSE, I forgot about a hyena's
EXCELLENT
sense of smell.

They can follow a trail for miles.
They can follow a scent that is days old.
They might even be better sniffers than dogs!

YOU'RE the only meaty thing in the herd — Ruby will **DEFINITELY** be able to sniff you out.

We need a better plan. And I have **JUST** the thing.

STEP SEVEN:
Look Un-Meaty

Like all good carnivores, hyenas love meaty meals.

If we make you look especially un-meaty, you could be safe.

Here are some options:

WORM

SKELETON

BROCCOLI

You look LOVELY in all the costumes — but which is best? Let's review what I know about a hyena's diet.

I know hyenas eat their **entire** dinners:

skin, hooves, horns, hair, guts . . .

ALL OF IT.

Their stomachs have a powerful acid that helps them

digest almost ANYTHING, even old stinky

meat that would poison most other animals.

Slimy, smelly, chewy, it's all delicious to a hyena.

I think Ruby might actually enjoy eating a worm,

so that idea is out.

Next, their jaws can
crunch RIGHT
THROUGH bone!
In fact, they even like
to eat bones.

Crusty crumpets!
That means the
skeleton definitely isn't
going to work.

GAG

You see, their heads and mouths aren't built like yours.

First, their heads are ENORMOUS.
Ruby's head might weigh 18 pounds (8 kg) —
that's probably twice as much as yours.

Next, their heads have POWERFUL MUSCLES
to give them one of the STRONGEST bites around.
In fact, their bite is so strong, their heads are specially
shaped so that their bite doesn't crack their own skull!

CARNASSIALS
(SHEARERS)

CANINES
(PIERCERS)

INCISORS
(RIPPERS)

BONE-CRUNCHING
PREMOLARS

And finally, their mouths are filled
with all sorts of teeth, including
HEAVY-DUTY BONE
CRUNCHERS.

I think the broccoli is the best choice.

Let me check with my **Encyclopedia
of Dangers and Perils,** just to
make sure I haven't forgotten
anything else.

Let me see, let me see . . .

Hurricane . . .

Hydrogen bomb . . .

Ah, here we go,

HYENAS!

"Hyenas love meaty dinners
but also eat fruits, eggs,
fish, snakes and . . .
BUGS."

HORRORS! No one is safe! Quick! Follow me!

STEP NINE:
Get in a Cage

Why didn't I think of this before! This birdcage is PERFECT.

The bars are beautiful and made of 100 PERCENT STEEL.

Ruby is getting close.

But don't be nervous.

I don't **THINK** she can chew
through those bars.

She's probably just **CURIOUS**.

Hyenas are very curious and very, very smart.
Especially when they work as a team.

When they work together, hyenas have the stamina and
smarts to accomplish almost anything . . .

. . . crack any puzzle . . . overturn
ANY obstacle.

Take it from me, NEVER
underestimate the
PROBLEM-SOLVING
BRAIN POWER
of hyenas.

Pretty much the ONLY thing
they can't do is CLIMB.

That's why leopards drag their dinner up into
trees — it's the only way to avoid having it
stolen by hyenas.

HEY!

I said there was safety in numbers!
WHERE DID YOU GO?

EVERY BUG FOR HERSELF!

CRASH!

PHEW! Another close escape!

I hope you'll join me again the next time a polite predator invites you to polka in the park or croquet on the lawn. With me at your side,

WHAT COULD POSSIBLY GO WRONG?

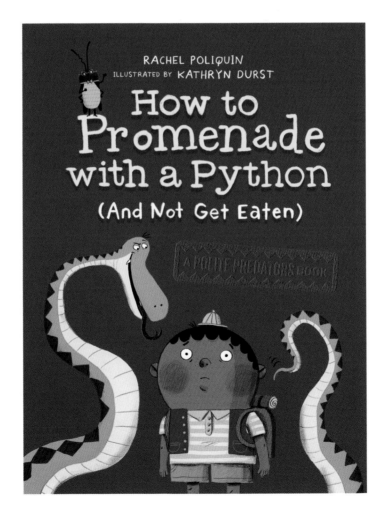

RACHEL POLIQUIN
ILLUSTRATED BY KATHRYN DURST

How to Promenade with a Python
(And Not Get Eaten)

A POLITE PREDATORS BOOK

RACHEL POLIQUIN writes about animals, mostly. She has written about ostriches, sled dogs, heroic moles and 800,000 jars of pickled fish. She is the author of the Polite Predators and Superpower Field Guide series, as well as *Beastly Puzzles: A Brain Boggling Animal Guessing Game*. She lives in Vancouver, Canada, with her husband and three children.

KATHRYN DURST has illustrated numerous children's books, including the Polite Predators series and the #1 *New York Times* bestseller from Paul McCartney, *Hey Grandude!* When she is not illustrating books, she can be found playing the accordion, growing vegetables, folk dancing or putting on shadow puppet shows. She lives in Toronto, Canada, with her grumpy mini dachshund named Chili Dog.